DOG TRAINING LOGBOOK

_____

DOG TRAINING LOG

Session Details

Date	Time	Location
Handler	Dog's Name	
Weather	Temperature	Additional Notes

Training

Type Of Training

Objective

Notes

Reward Used	Rating ☆ ☆ ☆ ☆ ☆

Map Out Training

TRAINING SESSION NOTES & THOUGHTS

DOG TRAINING LOG

Session Details

Date	Time	Location
Handler	Dog's Name	
Weather	Temperature	Additional Notes

Training

Type Of Training

Objective

Notes

Reward Used	Rating ☆ ☆ ☆ ☆ ☆

Map Out Training

TRAINING SESSION NOTES & THOUGHTS

DOG TRAINING LOG

Session Details

Date	Time	Location
Handler	Dog's Name	
Weather	Temperature	Additional Notes

Training

Type Of Training

Objective

Notes

Reward Used	Rating ☆ ☆ ☆ ☆ ☆

Map Out Training

TRAINING SESSION NOTES & THOUGHTS

DOG TRAINING LOG

Session Details

Date	Time	Location
Handler	Dog's Name	
Weather	Temperature	Additional Notes

Training

Type Of Training

Objective

Notes

Reward Used	Rating ☆ ☆ ☆ ☆ ☆

Map Out Training

TRAINING SESSION NOTES & THOUGHTS

DOG TRAINING LOG

Session Details

Date	Time	Location
Handler	Dog's Name	
Weather	Temperature	Additional Notes

Training

Type Of Training

Objective

Notes

Reward Used	Rating ☆ ☆ ☆ ☆ ☆

Map Out Training

TRAINING SESSION NOTES & THOUGHTS

DOG TRAINING LOG

Session Details

Date	Time	Location
Handler	Dog's Name	
Weather	Temperature	Additional Notes

Training

Type Of Training

Objective

Notes

Reward Used	Rating ☆ ☆ ☆ ☆ ☆

Map Out Training

TRAINING SESSION NOTES & THOUGHTS

DOG TRAINING LOG

Session Details

Date	Time	Location
Handler	Dog's Name	
Weather	Temperature	Additional Notes

Training

Type Of Training

Objective

Notes

Reward Used	Rating ☆ ☆ ☆ ☆ ☆

Map Out Training

TRAINING SESSION NOTES & THOUGHTS

DOG TRAINING LOG

Session Details

Date	Time	Location
Handler	Dog's Name	
Weather	Temperature	Additional Notes

Training

Type Of Training

Objective

Notes

Reward Used	Rating ☆ ☆ ☆ ☆ ☆

Map Out Training

TRAINING SESSION NOTES & THOUGHTS

DOG TRAINING LOG

Session Details

Date	Time	Location
Handler	Dog's Name	
Weather	Temperature	Additional Notes

Training

Type Of Training

Objective

Notes

Reward Used	Rating ☆ ☆ ☆ ☆ ☆

Map Out Training

TRAINING SESSION NOTES & THOUGHTS

DOG TRAINING LOG

Session Details

Date	Time	Location
Handler	Dog's Name	
Weather	Temperature	Additional Notes

Training

Type Of Training

Objective

Notes

Reward Used	Rating ☆ ☆ ☆ ☆ ☆

Map Out Training

TRAINING SESSION NOTES & THOUGHTS

DOG TRAINING LOG

Session Details

Date	Time	Location
Handler	Dog's Name	
Weather	Temperature	Additional Notes

Training

Type Of Training

Objective

Notes

Reward Used	Rating ☆ ☆ ☆ ☆ ☆

Map Out Training

TRAINING SESSION NOTES & THOUGHTS

DOG TRAINING LOG

Date	Time	Location
Handler	Dog's Name	
Weather	Temperature	Additional Notes

Training

Type Of Training

Objective

Notes

Reward Used	Rating ☆ ☆ ☆ ☆ ☆

Map Out Training

TRAINING SESSION NOTES & THOUGHTS

DOG TRAINING LOG

Session Details

Date	Time	Location
Handler	Dog's Name	
Weather	Temperature	Additional Notes

Training

Type Of Training

Objective

Notes

Reward Used	Rating ☆ ☆ ☆ ☆ ☆

Map Out Training

TRAINING SESSION NOTES & THOUGHTS

DOG TRAINING LOG

Session Details

Date	Time	Location
Handler	Dog's Name	
Weather	Temperature	Additional Notes

Training

Type Of Training

Objective

Notes

Reward Used	Rating ☆ ☆ ☆ ☆ ☆

Map Out Training

TRAINING SESSION NOTES & THOUGHTS

DOG TRAINING LOG

Session Details

Date	Time	Location
Handler	Dog's Name	
Weather	Temperature	Additional Notes

Training

Type Of Training

Objective

Notes

Reward Used	Rating ☆ ☆ ☆ ☆ ☆

Map Out Training

TRAINING SESSION NOTES & THOUGHTS

DOG TRAINING LOG

Session Details

Date	Time	Location
Handler	Dog's Name	
Weather	Temperature	Additional Notes

Training

Type Of Training

Objective

Notes

Reward Used	Rating ☆ ☆ ☆ ☆ ☆

Map Out Training

TRAINING SESSION NOTES & THOUGHTS

DOG TRAINING LOG

Session Details

Date	Time	Location
Handler	Dog's Name	
Weather	Temperature	Additional Notes

Training

Type Of Training

Objective

Notes

Reward Used	Rating ☆ ☆ ☆ ☆ ☆

Map Out Training

TRAINING SESSION NOTES & THOUGHTS

DOG TRAINING LOG

Session Details

Date	Time	Location
Handler	Dog's Name	
Weather	Temperature	Additional Notes

Training

Type Of Training

Objective

Notes

Reward Used	Rating ☆ ☆ ☆ ☆ ☆

Map Out Training

TRAINING SESSION NOTES & THOUGHTS

DOG TRAINING LOG

Session Details

Date	Time	Location
Handler	Dog's Name	
Weather	Temperature	Additional Notes

Training

Type Of Training

Objective

Notes

Reward Used	Rating ☆ ☆ ☆ ☆ ☆

Map Out Training

TRAINING SESSION NOTES & THOUGHTS

DOG TRAINING LOG

Session Details

Date	Time	Location
Handler	Dog's Name	
Weather	Temperature	Additional Notes

Training

Type Of Training

Objective

Notes

Reward Used	Rating ☆ ☆ ☆ ☆ ☆

Map Out Training

TRAINING SESSION NOTES & THOUGHTS

DOG TRAINING LOG

Session Details

Date	Time	Location
Handler	Dog's Name	
Weather	Temperature	Additional Notes

Training

Type Of Training

Objective

Notes

Reward Used	Rating ☆ ☆ ☆ ☆ ☆

Map Out Training

TRAINING SESSION NOTES & THOUGHTS

DOG TRAINING LOG

Session Details

Date	Time	Location
Handler	Dog's Name	
Weather	Temperature	Additional Notes

Training

Type Of Training

Objective

Notes

Reward Used	Rating ☆ ☆ ☆ ☆ ☆

Map Out Training

TRAINING SESSION NOTES & THOUGHTS

DOG TRAINING LOG

Session Details

Date	Time	Location
Handler	Dog's Name	
Weather	Temperature	Additional Notes

Training

Type Of Training

Objective

Notes

Reward Used	Rating ☆ ☆ ☆ ☆ ☆

Map Out Training

TRAINING SESSION NOTES & THOUGHTS

DOG TRAINING LOG

Session Details

Date	Time	Location
Handler	Dog's Name	
Weather	Temperature	Additional Notes

Training

Type Of Training

Objective

Notes

Reward Used	Rating ☆ ☆ ☆ ☆ ☆

Map Out Training

TRAINING SESSION NOTES & THOUGHTS

DOG TRAINING LOG

Session Details

Date	Time	Location
Handler	Dog's Name	
Weather	Temperature	Additional Notes

Training

Type Of Training

Objective

Notes

Reward Used	Rating ☆ ☆ ☆ ☆ ☆

Map Out Training

TRAINING SESSION NOTES & THOUGHTS

DOG TRAINING LOG

Session Details

Date	Time	Location
Handler	Dog's Name	
Weather	Temperature	Additional Notes

Training

Type Of Training

Objective

Notes

Reward Used	Rating ☆ ☆ ☆ ☆ ☆

Map Out Training

TRAINING SESSION NOTES & THOUGHTS

DOG TRAINING LOG

Session Details

Date	Time	Location
Handler	Dog's Name	
Weather	Temperature	Additional Notes

Training

Type Of Training

Objective

Notes

Reward Used	Rating ☆ ☆ ☆ ☆ ☆

Map Out Training

TRAINING SESSION NOTES & THOUGHTS

DOG TRAINING LOG

Session Details

Date	Time	Location
Handler	Dog's Name	
Weather	Temperature	Additional Notes

Training

Type Of Training

Objective

Notes

Reward Used	Rating ☆ ☆ ☆ ☆ ☆

Map Out Training

TRAINING SESSION NOTES & THOUGHTS

_____

_____

_____

_____

_____

_____

_____

_____

_____

_____

_____

_____

_____

_____

_____

_____

_____

_____

_____

_____

_____

_____

_____

DOG TRAINING LOG

Session Details

Date	Time	Location
Handler	Dog's Name	
Weather	Temperature	Additional Notes

Training

Type Of Training

Objective

Notes

Reward Used	Rating ☆ ☆ ☆ ☆ ☆

Map Out Training

TRAINING SESSION NOTES & THOUGHTS

DOG TRAINING LOG

Session Details

Date	Time	Location
Handler	Dog's Name	
Weather	Temperature	Additional Notes

Training

Type Of Training

Objective

Notes

Reward Used	Rating ☆ ☆ ☆ ☆ ☆

Map Out Training

TRAINING SESSION NOTES & THOUGHTS

DOG TRAINING LOG

Session Details

Date	Time	Location
Handler	Dog's Name	
Weather	Temperature	Additional Notes

Training

Type Of Training

Objective

Notes

Reward Used	Rating ☆ ☆ ☆ ☆ ☆

Map Out Training

TRAINING SESSION NOTES & THOUGHTS

DOG TRAINING LOG

Session Details

Date	Time	Location
Handler	Dog's Name	
Weather	Temperature	Additional Notes

Training

Type Of Training

Objective

Notes

Reward Used	Rating ☆ ☆ ☆ ☆ ☆

Map Out Training

TRAINING SESSION NOTES & THOUGHTS

DOG TRAINING LOG

Session Details

Date	Time	Location
Handler	Dog's Name	
Weather	Temperature	Additional Notes

Training

Type Of Training

Objective

Notes

Reward Used	Rating ☆ ☆ ☆ ☆ ☆

Map Out Training

TRAINING SESSION NOTES & THOUGHTS

DOG TRAINING LOG

Session Details

Date	Time	Location
Handler	Dog's Name	
Weather	Temperature	Additional Notes

Training

Type Of Training

Objective

Notes

Reward Used	Rating ☆ ☆ ☆ ☆ ☆

Map Out Training

TRAINING SESSION NOTES & THOUGHTS

DOG TRAINING LOG

Session Details

Date	Time	Location
Handler	Dog's Name	
Weather	Temperature	Additional Notes

Training

Type Of Training

Objective

Notes

Reward Used	Rating ☆ ☆ ☆ ☆ ☆

Map Out Training

TRAINING SESSION NOTES & THOUGHTS

DOG TRAINING LOG

Session Details

Date	Time	Location
Handler	Dog's Name	
Weather	Temperature	Additional Notes

Training

Type Of Training

Objective

Notes

Reward Used	Rating ☆ ☆ ☆ ☆ ☆

Map Out Training

TRAINING SESSION NOTES & THOUGHTS

DOG TRAINING LOG

Session Details

Date	Time	Location
Handler	Dog's Name	
Weather	Temperature	Additional Notes

Training

Type Of Training

Objective

Notes

Reward Used	Rating ☆ ☆ ☆ ☆ ☆

Map Out Training

TRAINING SESSION NOTES & THOUGHTS

DOG TRAINING LOG

Session Details

Date	Time	Location
Handler	Dog's Name	
Weather	Temperature	Additional Notes

Training

Type Of Training

Objective

Notes

Reward Used	Rating ☆ ☆ ☆ ☆ ☆

Map Out Training

TRAINING SESSION NOTES & THOUGHTS

DOG TRAINING LOG

Session Details

Date	Time	Location
Handler	Dog's Name	
Weather	Temperature	Additional Notes

Training

Type Of Training

Objective

Notes

Reward Used	Rating ☆ ☆ ☆ ☆ ☆

Map Out Training

TRAINING SESSION NOTES & THOUGHTS

DOG TRAINING LOG

Session Details

Date	Time	Location
Handler	Dog's Name	
Weather	Temperature	Additional Notes

Training

Type Of Training

Objective

Notes

Reward Used	Rating ☆ ☆ ☆ ☆ ☆

Map Out Training

TRAINING SESSION NOTES & THOUGHTS

DOG TRAINING LOG

Session Details

Date	Time	Location
Handler	Dog's Name	
Weather	Temperature	Additional Notes

Training

Type Of Training

Objective

Notes

Reward Used	Rating ☆ ☆ ☆ ☆ ☆

Map Out Training

TRAINING SESSION NOTES & THOUGHTS

DOG TRAINING LOG

Session Details

Date	Time	Location
Handler	Dog's Name	
Weather	Temperature	Additional Notes

Training

Type Of Training

Objective

Notes

Reward Used	Rating ☆ ☆ ☆ ☆ ☆

Map Out Training

TRAINING SESSION NOTES & THOUGHTS

DOG TRAINING LOG

Session Details

Date	Time	Location
Handler	Dog's Name	
Weather	Temperature	Additional Notes

Training

Type Of Training

Objective

Notes

Reward Used	Rating ☆ ☆ ☆ ☆ ☆

Map Out Training

TRAINING SESSION NOTES & THOUGHTS

DOG TRAINING LOG

Session Details

Date	Time	Location
Handler	Dog's Name	
Weather	Temperature	Additional Notes

Training

Type Of Training

Objective

Notes

Reward Used	Rating ☆ ☆ ☆ ☆ ☆

Map Out Training

TRAINING SESSION NOTES & THOUGHTS

DOG TRAINING LOG

Session Details

Date	Time	Location
Handler	Dog's Name	
Weather	Temperature	Additional Notes

Training

Type Of Training

Objective

Notes

Reward Used	Rating ☆ ☆ ☆ ☆ ☆

Map Out Training

TRAINING SESSION NOTES & THOUGHTS

DOG TRAINING LOG

Session Details

Date	Time	Location
Handler	Dog's Name	
Weather	Temperature	Additional Notes

Training

Type Of Training

Objective

Notes

Reward Used	Rating ☆ ☆ ☆ ☆ ☆

Map Out Training

TRAINING SESSION NOTES & THOUGHTS

DOG TRAINING LOG

Session Details

Date	Time	Location
Handler	Dog's Name	
Weather	Temperature	Additional Notes

Training

Type Of Training

Objective

Notes

Reward Used	Rating ☆ ☆ ☆ ☆ ☆

Map Out Training

TRAINING SESSION NOTES & THOUGHTS

DOG TRAINING LOG

Session Details

Date	Time	Location
Handler	Dog's Name	
Weather	Temperature	Additional Notes

Training

Type Of Training

Objective

Notes

Reward Used	Rating ☆ ☆ ☆ ☆ ☆

Map Out Training

TRAINING SESSION NOTES & THOUGHTS

DOG TRAINING LOG

Session Details

Date	Time	Location
Handler	Dog's Name	
Weather	Temperature	Additional Notes

Training

Type Of Training

Objective

Notes

Reward Used	Rating ☆ ☆ ☆ ☆ ☆

Map Out Training

TRAINING SESSION NOTES & THOUGHTS

_____

_____

_____

_____

_____

_____

_____

_____

_____

_____

_____

_____

_____

_____

_____

_____

_____

_____

_____

_____

_____

DOG TRAINING LOG

Session Details

Date	Time	Location
Handler	Dog's Name	
Weather	Temperature	Additional Notes

Training

Type Of Training

Objective

Notes

Reward Used	Rating ☆ ☆ ☆ ☆ ☆

Map Out Training

TRAINING SESSION NOTES & THOUGHTS

DOG TRAINING LOG

Session Details

Date	Time	Location
Handler	Dog's Name	
Weather	Temperature	Additional Notes

Training

Type Of Training

Objective

Notes

Reward Used	Rating ☆ ☆ ☆ ☆ ☆

Map Out Training

TRAINING SESSION NOTES & THOUGHTS

_____

_____

_____

_____

_____

_____

_____

_____

_____

_____

_____

_____

_____

_____

_____

_____

_____

_____

_____

_____

_____

_____

_____

DOG TRAINING LOG

Session Details		
Date	Time	Location
Handler	Dog's Name	
Weather	Temperature	Additional Notes

Training
Type Of Training
Objective
Notes

Reward Used	Rating ☆ ☆ ☆ ☆ ☆

Map Out Training

TRAINING SESSION NOTES & THOUGHTS

DOG TRAINING LOG

Session Details		
Date	Time	Location
Handler	Dog's Name	
Weather	Temperature	Additional Notes

Training

Type Of Training

Objective

Notes

Reward Used	Rating ☆ ☆ ☆ ☆ ☆

Map Out Training

TRAINING SESSION NOTES & THOUGHTS

DOG TRAINING LOG

Session Details

Date	Time	Location
Handler	Dog's Name	
Weather	Temperature	Additional Notes

Training

Type Of Training

Objective

Notes

Reward Used	Rating ☆ ☆ ☆ ☆ ☆

Map Out Training

TRAINING SESSION NOTES & THOUGHTS

DOG TRAINING LOG

Session Details

Date	Time	Location
Handler	Dog's Name	
Weather	Temperature	Additional Notes

Training

Type Of Training

Objective

Notes

Reward Used	Rating ☆ ☆ ☆ ☆ ☆

Map Out Training

Printed in Great Britain
by Amazon